LINCOLNESQUE

I0139478

John Strand

BROADWAY PLAY PUBLISHING INC
New York
www.broadwayplaypublishing.com
info@broadwayplaypublishing.com

LINCOLNESQUE
© Copyright 2007 John Strand

Cover photo by Craig Schwartz
First printing: April 2007
I S B N: 978-0-88145-335-5
Book design: Marie Donovan
Word processing: Microsoft Word
Typographic controls: Ventura Publisher
Typeface: Palatino
Printed and bound in the U S A

LINCOLNESQUE was commissioned by South Coast Repertory, Costa Mesa, California.

LINCOLNESQUE premiered at The Old Globe, San Diego, Calif., on 10 August 2006. The cast and creative contributors were as follows:

FRANCIS . . . . T Ryder Smith
LEO . . . . Leo Marks
SECRETARY OF WAR/DALY . . . . .James Sutorius
CARLA/DOCTOR . . . . .Magaly Colimon

Director . . . . .Joe Calarco
Scenic design . . . . Michael Fagin
Costumes . . . . Anne Kennedy
Sound . . . . Lindsay Jones
Lighting . . . . .Chris Rynne
Dramaturgy . . . . Jerry Patch

CHARACTERS & SETTING

FRANCIS, *tall, thin, later thirties*
LEO, *his younger brother; smaller, mid-thirties*
CARLA, *forty*
DALY, *older, near sixty*
SECRETARY OF WAR, *no fixed address; same age as* DALY
DOCTOR *in a psychiatric hospital*

The actor playing DALY *doubles as the* SECRETARY OF WAR.
The actor playing CARLA *doubles as the* DOCTOR.

There is a single set, multiple locations.

The play takes place in Washington, DC, in 2006.

A note: In the text, Abraham Lincoln's words, either from his speeches, letters, or personal writings, are always surrounded by quotes. This is intended as an aid to the actors.

Writing plays is an excellent way to go into debt, and I am not referring only to financial risk. I mean the better debt of gratitude owed to the artists and others who lend so much of their talent and time transforming the text into something alive and, one hopes, worthy. In San Diego at The Old Globe I owe special thanks to Joe Calarco for his vision and his expertise in achieving it, T Ryder Smith for thinking and caring to such an extraordinary degree, James Sutorius for being the word "professional" made flesh, Leo Marks for being So Damn Good, Magaly Colimon for her courage and spirit, Monica Cuoco and Cassidy Lubben for their grace and humor, Lou Spisto for his hospitality. In Miami at New Theatre, my thanks go to the irreplaceable Rafael de Acha for his wisdom and class, to Ricky J Martinez for his power and spirit, and to Eileen Suarez for her grace and warmth. At the Cleveland Play House, I thank Michael Bloom for his unwavering faith. Finally I acknowledge the debt I owe Jerry Patch, textualist nonpareil, a man who insists on living in a far land where ethics and honesty and keeping your word coexist with being very, very good at what you do. It is a rare place, and I am honored to be allowed to visit.

—J S

We must disenthrall ourselves, and then we shall save
our country.
—President Abraham Lincoln
Address to Congress, 1861

For Amanda

ACT ONE

Scene One

(A nearly empty stage. It is night. We are in a city square near Capitol Hill, Washington, DC, but there is nothing yet visible to tie us to a specific time and place. Enter slowly a man probably in his later thirties, tall and thin, dark unruly hair. He is dressed simply—dark trousers, white shirt—with the exception of the long dark coat with the large collar and lapels; rather 19th century. He takes the stance of an orator and begins to speak—or more accurately, to orate—and to gesture as if addressing a large outdoor gathering. Although he starts a bit hesitantly, it becomes evident during his speech that he honors, even savors the words he speaks, as if he were almost in love with the phrases.)

THE ORATOR: Ladies and gentlemen. Friends and supporters.

"If we could first know where we are, and wither we are tending, we could better judge what to do, and how to do it.

"We are now in the fifth year, since a policy was initiated, with the avowed object, and confident promise, of putting an end to slavery agitation.

"Under the operation of that policy, the agitation has not only not ceased, but it has constantly augmented.

"In my opinion, it will not cease, until a crisis shall have been reached, and passed.

"A house divided against itself cannot stand.

"I believe this government cannot endure,

permanently half slave and half free.

"I do not expect the union to be dissolved—I do not expect the house to fall—but I do expect it will cease to be divided.

"It will become all one thing, or all the other.

"The result is not doubtful. We shall not fail—if we stand firm, we shall not fail.

"Wise counsels may accelerate or mistakes delay it, but sooner or later the victory, my friends..."

(Another man has entered and stands, staring; this interrupts the speaker for a moment)

THE ORATOR: "The victory is sure to come."

(This other man is smaller, a few years younger. He is clean-shaven and his clothes are unmistakably contemporary, though boring and conservative, not to mention frumpled and ill-fitting)

LEO: Do you realize what time it is?

THE ORATOR: June, 1858.

LEO: I am not in the mood. It's 11:15. I could hear you all the way from the Starbucks on the corner.

THE ORATOR: That far?

LEO: Take off the coat.

THE ORATOR: Leo—

LEO: Take off the coat. People live in this neighborhood. And presumably, they try to sleep in this neighborhood.

THE ORATOR: *(Taking off the coat)* I'm sorry, Leo. Are you just getting home from work?

LEO: I've been walking around for the last half hour trying to find you.

THE ORATOR: It's a lovely night for a walk.

LEO: You promised me, Francis. You promised you wouldn't leave the apartment when I'm gone.

FRANCIS: I can't give my speech in an apartment, Leo. The other tenants knock on the walls.

LEO: I am legally responsible for you. What would Doctor Barlow say if she could see this?

FRANCIS: She would sigh disapprovingly.

LEO: I can't trust you, is that it? I can't trust you not to get into trouble when I'm gone?

FRANCIS: I'm not in trouble.

(The blue light of a police vehicle, perhaps the crackle of a police radio dispatch)

LEO: Oh great! Here we go again. This is so humiliating. God dammit, Francis. Do you have identification with you?

FRANCIS: Leo. I think they should be able to recognize the president of the United States.

(They both stare at the approaching officer, off. Lights down. Transition...)

Scene Two

(Lights come back up on LEO, *alone, downstage. The poor guy. He hasn't got a clue. The multiple flaws in his personal grooming and general appearance indicate a mind that is almost exclusively engaged in work and only occasionally in the real world.)*

LEO: This city eats people. It's a dirty secret, carefully guarded. Big bites of human flesh, right here in our nation's capital, the city carnivorous. People come here, healthy, normal. Full of ideals. Convinced they're going to change things, make the world a better place. That's how I was, once. Then they start to lose whole parts of themselves. Their backbones. Their brains. Their balls—forgive me. I don't mean to be graphic. But the truly frightening thing is, the victims won't even discuss it. Too busy, too locked into the battle... Devoured. That's what happened to my brother.

(He now joins FRANCIS *in the waiting room of a city-run psychiatric clinic.)*

LEO: Francis. I want to ask you a favor.

FRANCIS: Yes.

LEO: One favor.

FRANCIS: Yes.

LEO: Focus. Can you do that for me?

FRANCIS: Yes.

LEO: When you focus, you're capable of anything.

FRANCIS: Am I?

LEO: You're the equal of anyone. There's nothing you can't do when you focus. So I want you to focus.

FRANCIS: I will, then. Splendid. *(A beat)* Focus on what, Leo?

LEO: On here and now. This place and time. And what we're facing. Can you do that?

FRANCIS: Of course.

LEO: Good. Fix your collar. In back. Why didn't you shave?

FRANCIS: I did.

LEO: Did you brush?

FRANCIS: Yes.

LEO: They watch for things like that.

FRANCIS: Like what?

LEO: Poor hygiene. It's an indicator of depression. Do you know what you're going to say?

FRANCIS: I'm not supposed to prepare.

LEO: Oh Francis, no. *They* prepare.

FRANCIS: They do?

LEO: Of course they do. All psychiatrists prepare.

FRANCIS: Oh.

LEO: Damn.

FRANCIS: What should I do now?

LEO: It's my fault.

FRANCIS: It's not your fault, Leo.

LEO: I should have taken the time to create some mock scenarios. Now you're walking in there blind, and it's my fault.

FRANCIS: You cannot be faulted, Leo. I'll be fine. I plan to be honest.

LEO: But what do *they* plan to be? And what if the police bring charges? "Uttering racial slurs in public."

FRANCIS: People are frightened by the word "slavery".

LEO: "Disturbing the peace" I can understand. But you were reciting an historical speech, word for word. Was it word for word?

FRANCIS: Yes.

LEO: One misdemeanor charge and they can revoke your outpatient status. I hope you realize that.
(He looks at his watch.)

FRANCIS: Are you late for something?

LEO: No.

FRANCIS: You looked at your watch.

LEO: I'm just checking.

FRANCIS: You don't have time.

LEO: I've got time.

FRANCIS: If you're busy, I understand, Leo.

LEO: I'm not busy, all right? I have a staff meeting at two. I'll have to take a cab, that's all. *(A beat)* Where are they? What's taking so long? Are you relaxed?

FRANCIS: Yes.

LEO: Just relax.

FRANCIS: I am relaxed.

LEO: And remember this: You haven't done anything wrong.

FRANCIS: That's not true.

LEO: I mean recently.

FRANCIS: That's not true either.

LEO: I wish they'd let me come in there with you.

FRANCIS: I'm more relaxed without you.

LEO: Thanks a lot.

FRANCIS: Don't take umbrage, Leo.

LEO: No. No. "Umbrage" is on the list.

FRANCIS: I apologize.

LEO: *Please* don't start using the words on the list.

FRANCIS: O K.

LEO: Please, Francis. I can't help you if you won't help yourself.

FRANCIS: It may be that you can't help me, full stop.

LEO: Oh Jesus... All right. Let's change the subject.

FRANCIS: I should be the one helping *you*, Leo.
I'm your elder brother.

LEO: "Older brother."

FRANCIS: I have disappointed you.

LEO: I'm not disappointed.

FRANCIS: But I too have suffered a disappointment
to my ambitions.

LEO: We're going to talk about the here and now,
Francis. We're not talking about ambitions or battles
or casualties or anything like that. All right?

FRANCIS: Yes.

LEO: You're doing so well lately. You're making
progress. We will not go backwards. I won't let that
happen.

FRANCIS: Thank you, Leo.

LEO: What are your hobbies? What are your interests?

FRANCIS: Cleaning.

LEO: Cleaning is your job, it's not your hobby.

FRANCIS: Cooking.

LEO: Cooking, good. What type of cuisine?

FRANCIS: American traditional.

LEO: All right. What else?

FRANCIS: History.

LEO: Francis.

FRANCIS: What's wrong with history?

LEO: Stick to the here and now. Please. What else?

FRANCIS: Well. Politics.

LEO: No.

FRANCIS: It interests me, that's all.

LEO: If you bring it up, they can go there—and take you with them. Just avoid it. Talk about your job. What about the job, anyway?

FRANCIS: It's all right.

LEO: How long has it been?

FRANCIS: This is the third week.

LEO: That's good. What do you do?

FRANCIS: I clean.

LEO: I know, but clean what?

FRANCIS: Bathrooms, primarily. Also hallways. I'm going to do buffer training. Then I can buff.

LEO: On your own?

FRANCIS: Under observation, at first.

LEO: You don't talk to anyone, I hope. Because we can't afford for you to lose this job.

FRANCIS: I rarely converse.

LEO: Good. It's safer. What's the building like?

FRANCIS: Typical Washington. Full of lawyers.

LEO: How do they treat you?

FRANCIS: Like lawyers.

LEO: Are they mean to you?

FRANCIS: They pretend not to see me.

LEO: Because if any of them are rude to you, I want you to tell me. Or if they make jokes. That falls under workplace harassment. *(A beat; he looks at his brother a moment; meaningfully)* Do you really hate it?

FRANCIS: Yes. I hate it.

LEO: I'm sorry, Francis.

FRANCIS: It's not your fault.

LEO: It's got to be better than St. Elizabeth's.

FRANCIS: Anything is better than St. Elizabeth's.

LEO: *(Picturing it)* Yeah.

(A beat, as they both picture it)

FRANCIS: I don't want to go back there, Leo.

LEO: We're not going back there. As long as we keep making progress. I don't care if we measure it in millimeters, as long as it's progress. Am I right?

FRANCIS: Yes.

LEO: We've gone from a psychiatric hospital to a building full of lawyers.

FRANCIS: Is that progress?

LEO: Yes! From here we get you back on your feet. You settle into this job. Later we find you something more at your level. You put some money aside, get your own apartment. We reduce your medication. Before you know it, we're back to square one. We've been through so much, Francis.

FRANCIS: Yes.

LEO: What's a building full of lawyers after what we've been through?

FRANCIS: A peccadillo.

LEO: A pecc— *(He lets it go.)* All you have to do is focus.

(A beat)

FRANCIS: I find it ironic, though.

LEO: What?

FRANCIS: Some of my most remarkable accomplishments were in law.

LEO: Francis.

FRANCIS: I don't mean to upset you, Leo. But if they knew who was mopping up their little yellow urine stains—

LEO: Don't, Francis.

FRANCIS: They'd be shocked speechless.

LEO: Francis—

FRANCIS: The sixteenth president of the United States.

LEO: Stop it! *(A beat)* This isn't going to work, is it?

FRANCIS: It can work, Leo.

LEO: *(Almost letting the rage loose)* Not! Not! If you don't *want* it to work!

FRANCIS: I want it to work. But on my terms. Their terms—that's what doesn't work, Leo. It never has.

LEO: *(Despairing)* Oh God.

FRANCIS: And you know it as well as I. You just haven't found the courage to face it, that's all.

LEO: "Courage"?

FRANCIS: The term is apt. Will you not admit it?

LEO: Francis, when you go away, into wherever it is you go—you go away from me, too. Do I deserve that?

FRANCIS: I'm sorry, Leo. We are both of us casualties of the war.

LEO: *(With an effort, calmer now)* I'm sorry I lost my temper.

FRANCIS: It is forgotten. *(A beat)* I will not abandon you. You need me.

LEO: Do I?

FRANCIS: To help you find the courage. My goal is your emancipation.

LEO: Can we keep that between us?

FRANCIS: Understood.

LEO: Let's not tell the examiner.

FRANCIS: Understood. *(A beat)* Have you been doing your breathing?

LEO: When I have time.

FRANCIS: You must do your breathing exercises. Promise me. Leo.

LEO: I promise.

FRANCIS: It will help with your speech impediment.

LEO: I don't have a speech impediment, I have picked up a temporary, minor stutter. Occasionally. When I'm nervous or intimidated. Can we maintain focus here, please? This is about you, not me.

(A beat)

FRANCIS: Leo? Will you do me one kindness before I go in there?

LEO: What.

FRANCIS: Call me Abe? Just once?

LEO: I won't, Francis.

FRANCIS: What would it cost you?

LEO: What would it cost *you*, that's the issue.

FRANCIS: Just say it quickly. "Good luck, Abe."

LEO: Don't do this to me.

FRANCIS: Shake my hand.

LEO: Don't, Francis.

FRANCIS: "Godspeed, Mister President."

LEO: No.

FRANCIS: It will relax me. Please? Please, Leo?

(A beat)

LEO: No.

FRANCIS: *(Spurned and hurt)* I admire your firmness.

LEO: One of us has to keep a grip. If we both let go...

FRANCIS: Understood.

LEO: I'm thinking of you.

FRANCIS: Understood.

LEO: I am determined to help you fight this. I am thinking of *your* well-being. *(A beat; audible sigh)* "Mister President."

(FRANCIS looks at his brother, takes a deep breath, seems to draw strength from the air around him.)

FRANCIS: May I tell you something, Leo? I love you. *(A beat)* And I think you would make an excellent cabinet secretary.

(LEO, not at all amused, shakes his head, a gesture of hopelessness. He looks like he might cry. FRANCIS stands, looking off)

FRANCIS: I believe they're ready for me. And I for them.

(Lights change as FRANCIS takes a few steps downstage. LEO remains seated a moment, looks again at his watch, exits as FRANCIS begins his testimony)

FRANCIS: Gentlemen. "If we could first know where we are, and wither we are tending, we could better judge what to do, and how to do it." But where are we? And who? The thing is, I am a house divided against itself. I do not say the house will fall. But I will cease to be divided. I will be all one thing—a floor-buffer on probation—or all the other—the Shakespeare of American politics, reincarnate. "Without the assistance of the Divine Being, I cannot succeed; with it, I cannot fail." Gentlemen, I see that you are casualties in the present war and suffer terribly. Take heart: my administration shall do its utmost to bring the conflict to a swift conclusion. Are there any questions? *(There are none.)* Then I thank you for coming to see me, and bid you good day.

(He turns to go, but encounters a middle-aged man. This is someone who appears to have suffered a serious reversal of fortune. He has a deeply wonkish look. He wears one of those ubiquitous Washington trench coats, soiled; he has slept in these clothes for a few weeks now, although he means to do a laundry soon, when he has the free time. His large, thick eyeglasses make his watery eyes look like two fish in fishbowl. He carries a battered briefcase, overflowing with papers, spreadsheets, newspaper clippings. He is not a derelict, not really. Despite the breakdown and the loss of employment, the nights spent in transient hotels and shelters, the days spent wandering city parks and the Metro, he retains something of his dignity. In his friend Francis he has recognized a kindred spirit)

SECRETARY OF WAR: Mister President.

FRANCIS: Edwin M Stanton, my secretary of war. What news, Ed?

SECRETARY OF WAR: We were supposed to meet in the park.

FRANCIS: I was delayed. An important address to the leaders of Congress.

SECRETARY OF WAR: I was wondering, Mister President, if you could loan me a couple of dollars till I get back on my feet.

FRANCIS: *(Searching his pockets unsuccessfully)* The national economy is in distress.

SECRETARY OF WAR: If I could eat something and keep it down, it would really help clear my head.

FRANCIS: Come with me, Edwin. A cabinet secretary should not be in want.

SECRETARY OF WAR: *(The thought halts him.)* You're not planning to give another speech, are you?

FRANCIS: Not at present.

SECRETARY OF WAR: God bless you, Honest Abe. Let's go.

FRANCIS: The war rages on, Edwin. It pains me beyond expression, to look out upon the city and see the many victims.

SECRETARY OF WAR: Oh, I hear you there. Victims, everywhere you look.

FRANCIS: Do you realize I have lost all confidence in my generals?

SECRETARY OF WAR: Military spending as an inflation-adjusted percentage of the gross domestic product has realized multiple consecutive years of accelerated growth rivaled only by energy costs. Plus, they secretly put powerful hormones in the food supply. Did I tell you that, Abe?

FRANCIS: Yes, Edwin, you did.

SECRETARY OF WAR: You know who controls the American food supply? Lockheed-Martin.

(FRANCIS begins to exit; The SECRETARY OF WAR follows.)

SECRETARY OF WAR: The American electorate is being drugged, Abe. How else do you explain the last two presidential elections?

(They exit.)

Scene Three

(Office corridor, Capitol Hill office building. LEO comes downstage and addresses the audience.)

LEO: Walking. In other parts of the country, an innocent act of locomotion. Here, though, in the halls of government, stride is an indicator of your personal power quotient.

(Enter a woman, forties but convinced it doesn't show. This is CARLA, the newly hired chief of staff. She carries a manila folder thick with papers. She crosses importantly, loudly. After she exits:)

LEO: Every footstep a hammer blow that proclaims: "I am busy, I am important, I am essential to the security of the nation."

(Re-enter CARLA, crossing. She halts. There is something arresting about her, in the sense of "state trooper." She would describe herself as "focused." Some of her colleagues would say "vicious," but not within ear shot)

CARLA: *(To LEO, unfriendly)* Hey.

LEO: *(Still to us)* You know, I never had a speech impediment before I started working up here.

CARLA: Are you the one who wanted to see me?

LEO: *(To us)* The words used to just flow.

CARLA: I've got maybe four minutes, so whatever it is it better be important and it better be quick.

LEO: The speech—the draft—I left it on your chair.

CARLA: Was that from you?

LEO: Yes.

CARLA: Number one: don't enter my office when I'm not in it. Number two: don't put something on my chair unless you want me to sit on it. Number three: We're ten points down in the polls and you want Dave to devote a whole speech to re-districting?

LEO: It's so important, Carla—

CARLA: Nobody understands redistricting. I don't understand it.

LEO: It's very simple.

CARLA: So I'm stupid?

LEO: No, but see, under the present proposal, we lose twenty-two precincts that we carried with an average vote of sixty percent the last three elections—

CARLA: Beltway.

LEO: —in exchange for an upper-white-collar demographic that voted fifty-two to fifty-five percent *against* us—

CARLA: It reads Beltway, Larry.

LEO: It's Leo.

CARLA: Re-districting is a Beltway issue.

LEO: But Dave asked me directly—

CARLA: We're not going there.

LEO: I think that's a mistake, Carla.

CARLA: I'm not interested in what you think. I'm interested in getting Dave Carpenter re-elected to congress, which is why they brought me on. I intend to clear out the dead wood around here, and unless you show me otherwise, you're kindling.

LEO: What, are you—? Are you threatening to fire me?

CARLA: Yeah.

LEO: I am Dave's top speech writer. Dave hired me himself—

CARLA: The people that Dave hired himself got us ten points down in the polls. It's crisis time. Incumbents are not supposed to lose elections, and I am not about to preside over a disgrace. Get my message?

LEO: Yes.

CARLA: Good. I expect you to get on the stick. You're older, you've been around the block.

LEO: I'm not "older", what do you mean?

CARLA: What is that? Is that a speech impediment?

LEO: No.

CARLA: We've got a speechwriter with a speech impediment? *(Heavenward)* Is there some kind of joke being played around there that I should know about? *(To LEO)* Can't you get treatment for that or something? I mean, think how that *looks*. *(She starts to leave, halts.)* Wait a minute: Do you have a brother?

LEO: *(Caught off guard)* Do I have a brother?

CARLA: You're the one with the whiz-kid brother who lost it, right?

LEO: What's that got to do with me?

CARLA: It all makes sense now. Forget it.

LEO: You're insinuating that there's something wrong with me because of my brother.

CARLA: Am I?

LEO: My brother is private. What happened to him is private.

CARLA: I'll take the speechwriting from here.

LEO: You? But you don't have a clue about—I mean, you've only been up here a few weeks.

CARLA: I'm going with something lighter in tone. More humorous, throw in a few jokes.

LEO: Dave isn't known for humor.

CARLA: What's he known for?

LEO: Steadiness. Reliability.

CARLA: And boring suits. No wonder we're ten points down.

LEO: Dave can't do humor.

CARLA: He's never had the chance. Not with the stuff *you* write for him.

LEO: You're making a huge mistake, Carla.

CARLA: No, Sweetheart, I am fixing a huge mistake.

LEO: Dave is not Jay Leno.

CARLA: Really? Any other revelations?

LEO: People laugh *at* politicians, they don't laugh *with* them. And you do not have the right to call me "sweetheart".

(CARLA *gives him a smile and exits in one direction;* LEO *remains a moment, does his breathing exercises, which do not seem to help, then exits angrily in the other direction.*)

Scene Four

(*Lights up on* FRANCIS *and the* SECRETARY OF WAR *at* LEO's *apartment. The* SECRETARY OF WAR *is busy rearranging the chaos overflowing from his briefcase*)

FRANCIS: "Couch and Smith, Stanton! Why am I plagued with Couch and Smith? Smith took ten days to move his army from Carlisle to Hagerstown. That's not

an inch over fifty-five miles, if so much. While General
Meade, with twenty-thousand veteran troops, sits by
and lets Lee's army build bridges over the river and slip
away at his leisure without attacking him. I believe you
do not appreciate the magnitude of the misfortune
involved in Lee's escape."

SECRETARY OF WAR: *(Distracted)* No, I totally appreciate
it... Did you move my spreadsheets?

FRANCIS: "He was within our easy grasp and to have
closed upon him would have ended the war. Now the
war will be prolonged indefinitely."

SECRETARY OF WAR: Yes. That sucks.

FRANCIS: "Our golden opportunity is gone, and I am
distressed immeasurably because of it."

SECRETARY OF WAR: You are? Abe. Come on, now.
Don't get down. Come here.

(A warm hug from the SECRETARY OF WAR)

FRANCIS: Thank you, Edwin.

SECRETARY OF WAR: Let's see a smile. Come on.

(FRANCIS smiles)

SECRETARY OF WAR: There you go, that's the spirit.
You can't let the bastards get you down. So what if
there's one on every damn street corner? *(Darkly)* Knife-
wielding, venom-spitting, flesh-eating bastards from
the darkest parking garages of hell. *(Returning)* Avoid
'em. Focus on the future. What's the future hold for
you, Abe?

FRANCIS: Well. I'm going to free the slaves. And win the
war.

SECRETARY OF WAR: There you go.

FRANCIS: Then I'm going to be assassinated.

SECRETARY OF WAR: I'm thinking about going into consulting. Open my own office until they contact me for a position at Treasury or the World Bank... Oh, man.

FRANCIS: Edwin?

SECRETARY OF WAR: My head again. Mister President...

(FRANCIS *takes out a vial of pills, offers it to his* SECRETARY OF WAL, *who takes one or more and swallows*)

SECRETARY OF WAR: I think I need to lie down here for a minute. If anyone calls... I'm unavailable. *(He lies down and sleeps)*

FRANCIS: Sleep, my good secretary. A grateful nation thanks you.

(Lights lower as FRANCIS *sits and settles into the Lincoln Memorial pose.)*

(After a beat, LEO *now returns home)*

LEO: Francis? Francis, are you asleep?

FRANCIS: No.

(Lights back up low)

LEO: You were just sitting here in the dark. *(Discovering his companion)* Who the hell is this?

FRANCIS: My secretary of war.

LEO: You know I don't want strangers in the apartment when I'm not home.

FRANCIS: Never strangers, but friends.

LEO: Street people are not safe, Francis. Is he asleep? God, he stinks, too.

FRANCIS: It is my policy to receive at the White House.

LEO: I said no.

FRANCIS: Americans of every class and persuasion, come to see their president.

LEO: Not tonight, Francis, please. I'm too tired.

FRANCIS: You would be heartened, Leo, to hear their simple desires and honest complaints.

LEO: No I wouldn't. And he's not staying here tonight.

FRANCIS: Wherefore does a government exist, if not to comfort its citizens?

LEO: I got you the shrimp lo mein.

FRANCIS: No dumplings?

LEO: You wanted dumplings?

FRANCIS: It is of no importance. The Union soldiers on the front are living on hard tack and biscuits.

LEO: You're not doing very well tonight, are you.

FRANCIS: I disagree.

LEO: If one more person disagrees with me today, I'm going to break something.

FRANCIS: You are troubled.

LEO: Things are falling apart at work.

FRANCIS: Tell me.

LEO: Dave gave a speech on Sunday—with "humor." It tanked. We're now fifteen points down in the polls.

FRANCIS: Were you its author?

LEO: No. Carla, new chief of staff. Comes from corporate, like that's supposed to be impressive. She doesn't even know how much she doesn't know.

FRANCIS: I myself had no formal education to speak of, growing up in the Indiana bottomland. Is the broccoli chicken spicy?

LEO: Very.

(FRANCIS *declines*.)

LEO: He's blowing it, Francis. He's dead in the water. A month from now, I'll be out of a job again.

FRANCIS: Providence extends its hand.

LEO: I didn't follow that.

FRANCIS: An opportunity to escape the misery of your own making.

LEO: I'm not miserable.

FRANCIS: Your spirit has been depleted by the ravages of hypocrisy and corruption with which our nation's capital has ever been plagued.

LEO: You know, Francis? Having a conversation with you is always kind of an adventure.

FRANCIS: Thank you. I'll have a spring roll, if I may.

LEO: So my spirit is depleted?

FRANCIS: As dry as a stream bed in August.

LEO: So what should I do?

FRANCIS: Lay down your arms and go home. You are in rebellion against yourself.

LEO: It's that simple, huh?

FRANCIS: Your mind is confused.

LEO: *My* mind is confused?

FRANCIS: A simple decision is required. Leave Washington, the source of all your woe.

LEO: And all my income. Who'll pay the rent? Or buy your medication?

FRANCIS: You will learn some honest trade and start anew.

LEO: Oh. Just like that.

FRANCIS: A school teacher.

LEO: Me?

FRANCIS: You would excel. Public service and education, your two passions.

LEO: You know what school teachers make?

FRANCIS: We will travel back to Illinois, where the expense of living is less.

LEO: You've never set foot in Illinois.

FRANCIS: I don't wish to see you suffer any longer, Leo.

LEO: Yeah. Thanks.

FRANCIS: And you wouldn't be fifteen points down if you repositioned Carpenter to get maximum separation on E & I.

(LEO *stares at him; a beat*)

LEO: Where did that come from?

FRANCIS: It is my observation.

LEO: Is that Francis talking? Former king of the Hill staffers? Or is that you, Mister Lincoln? E & I. Ethics and integrity.

FRANCIS: Your man needs to leave the low road of partisan politics and gain the high road of moral rectitude. His opponent will not follow, for he does not know the terrain.

LEO: And that's supposed to win the election?

FRANCIS: The land itself has a depleted spirit, Leo. It is everywhere apparent. The people hunger for heroes.

LEO: Heroes.

FRANCIS: Leaders who act with courage in the interests of the nation.

LEO: Preferably tall? With a beard and a stovepipe hat?

FRANCIS: The common man needs inspiration.

LEO: Dave, inspiring? You'd need a magician, not a speechwriter.

FRANCIS: Let him grow whiskers.

LEO: Dave? With a beard?

FRANCIS: Let his words be taller and he shall be, too.

LEO: I've been trying to get him to take a stance on corporate fraud and government waste in federal contracting—you know, Iraq, the Gulf Coast. You look at the numbers and it's a unifier issue, cuts right across party lines, income, education—

(A beat; he stares at his brother, who continues to eat calmly.)

LEO: What am I doing? I'm not even supposed to *mention* politics to you. Doctor Barlow warned us.

FRANCIS: Doctor Barlow is a charlatan and a rebel.

LEO: *(A beat)* Moral what-did-you-say?

FRANCIS: Rectitude.

LEO: So just theoretically, now: how would Dave go about projecting...?

FRANCIS: The correct phrases, to begin with.

LEO: What, lines from Lincoln?

FRANCIS: Altered and updated.

LEO: Plagiarized.

FRANCIS: Adapted.

LEO: Stolen.

FRANCIS: Borrowed. And expertly disguised. I've jotted a few down. I could show you.

LEO: *(He wants to, but...)* No. No way. It's too dangerous. You'll get all flipped out, like before.

FRANCIS: Do I appear to you "all flipped out"?

LEO: They'll put you on stronger medication. You can't tolerate the dose you're on now.

FRANCIS: I have resolved the tolerance issue.

LEO: What do you mean?

FRANCIS: I donate my pills to the needy.

LEO: What?

FRANCIS: *(The sleeping man)* Secretary Stanton.

LEO: Francis.

FRANCIS: His need is far greater than mine.

LEO: That's illegal.

FRANCIS: A technicality of law.

LEO: You're on probation. If you get arrested again—

FRANCIS: I have taken no medicine for more than a week.

LEO: You stopped taking your medication?

FRANCIS: It stupefied my faculties.

LEO: You're not taking *anything*!?

FRANCIS: I no longer need it.

LEO: Does Doctor Barlow know about this?

FRANCIS: I've not volunteered the information.

LEO: Think of the risk you're taking.

FRANCIS: Her treatment was the greater risk.

LEO: You can't go through another breakdown, Francis.

FRANCIS: What you mean is, *you* cannot go through another breakdown.

LEO: All right, *I* can't. Seeing you strapped in that bed. The screaming.

FRANCIS: We shall not have to endure it, for it will not come to pass.

LEO: Oh. Suddenly you're cured?

FRANCIS: I am not ill.

LEO: Francis. Can we be honest here for a minute?

FRANCIS: "Honest" is my nickname.

LEO: Look at me. You're not sick?

FRANCIS: I have heard no voices for many months now.

LEO: Three.

FRANCIS: Four. I am ever as well as you.

LEO: As well as me.

FRANCIS: Better, in fact.

LEO: I didn't assault two uniformed security guards a year ago. I didn't have a major psychotic incident in a Capitol Hill office in front of dozens of co-workers. I didn't spend six months in a psychiatric hospital.

FRANCIS: I suffered a disappointment to my ambitions.

LEO: Francis. You think you're Lincoln.

FRANCIS: Untrue. I know I am Lincoln.

LEO: Jesus...

FRANCIS: And I am in better health than you, brother, for I have escaped.

LEO: I've heard this, Francis—

FRANCIS: The obsession, the sixteen-hour work days-

LEO: I've heard it all before.

FRANCIS: —the soul-destroying rejection of honor and principle. The lies, Leo. The public deceptions and private delusions. I have climbed from the stinking pit and walked away. You are on the bottom still, and digging deeper.

LEO: So I should climb out?

FRANCIS: I extend my hand to you.

LEO: And I should live like you?

FRANCIS: I am happy. Are you happy, Leo?

LEO: No. I'm not happy. But at least I'm still sane! Face the facts. You hide inside this character of yours— Abraham fucking Lincoln! It's not even original! —And how am I supposed to be "happy" when I spend all my free time taking care of my older brother instead of having normal healthy relationships with normal healthy people and you should be goddam grateful that I work this job, because without it you'd be right back in Saint Elizabeth's! *(A long beat; the storm is over)* O K, I'm sorry. Francis?

FRANCIS: No.

LEO: I'm tired. I didn't mean that.

FRANCIS: No. You meant it. You resent me.

LEO: I don't resent you.

FRANCIS: You have no life at all, and I am the cause.

LEO: You're not the cause.

FRANCIS: Then I am the excuse, and that is worse. We are both of us failures at life, Leo. So we live for our work.

LEO: Francis, look—

FRANCIS: Politics is a substitute for family. For love. Even sex.

LEO: *(Meaning "not entirely")* That's not true.

FRANCIS: It's shameful. Behold the emptiness. I blame myself.

LEO: It's not your fault.

FRANCIS: When mother died, she made us promise always to take care of one another. I have not done my share. And that has not been very presidential of me.

LEO: She was in such pain, we'd have promised her anything.

FRANCIS: Now you're the one in pain.

LEO: Oh God...

FRANCIS: I think the thing is clear. I must find a way to set you free.

LEO: Francis.

FRANCIS: Here is my proposal. I shall provide you the phrases that inspire the populace. You will employ them to help your man win his race.

LEO: Dave? No one can help him win that race.

FRANCIS: When he wins, you will quit this city, and I with you. We will return to Illinois, where we belong. Is it agreed?

LEO: First of all, he won't win. And second, I don't know anyone in Illinois. After Dave loses, I'll scramble around here, pick up something with one of the federal agencies.

FRANCIS: You will despise it.

LEO: *(A beat)* You're right.

FRANCIS: Better to go out a winner and leave on your own terms. Are we agreed?

LEO: Francis.

FRANCIS: Good. We are agreed. We shall keep my role secret. The credit will be yours.

LEO: Yeah, or the blame. This is nuts, even for you. A couple of recycled Lincoln phrases stuck inside a speech are not going to get Dave Carpenter re-elected. *(A beat)* Did you save me a spring roll?

(A guilty look from FRANCIS*)*

LEO: That was not very presidential of you.

FRANCIS: I shall have the secretary of war look into it.

(The SECRETARY OF WAR *awakens grouchily.)*

SECRETARY OF WAR: Hey. Can you keep it down? *(Meaning* LEO*)* What's he doing at a Cabinet meeting?

FRANCIS: This is my brother Leo, Edwin.

SECRETARY OF WAR: What's that smell? Is that him?

FRANCIS: Chinese. Will you dine with us?

SECRETARY OF WAR: No, no. M S G. Lockheed-Martin.

(He returns to sleep. Lights. Transition)

Scene Five.

*(*LEO, *back at the congressional offices. Enter* CARLA, *in her customary hurry)*

CARLA: He shouldn't shave?

LEO: Right.

CARLA: Dave Carpenter should grow a beard?

LEO: And we should take away his neckties.

CARLA: What, suicide prevention?

LEO: Image make-over. We're fifteen points down.

CARLA: I know how far down we are.

LEO: We need to do something unexpected.

CARLA: You know what really irks me about you?

LEO: Am I required to answer that?

CARLA: Give it a shot.

LEO: Everything?

CARLA: You're so damn smug. So say it. "I told you so." Go ahead.

LEO: What good will that do?

CARLA: You are so smug.

LEO: O K, O K. "I told you so." There.

CARLA: Oh. Rub it in.

LEO: Carla—

CARLA: Fine. I screwed up. Dave is boring, but I made him ridiculous. I personally dropped us five points in the polls. My ex-husband warned me to stay in corporate. I hate it when he's right. Maybe I should just resign.

LEO: You don't need to resign, Carla.

CARLA: No?

LEO: No. As soon as Dave loses, we'll all be fired.

CARLA: You know, I actually thought that maybe— just maybe—it was going to be inspiring up here. Capitol Hill. History and all that shit.

LEO: Changing the course of human events.

CARLA: Yeah. Heroic. Maybe even sexy. Ha.

LEO: Ha.

CARLA: Like those television shows where everybody is so brilliant and beautiful.

LEO: Pure fiction.

CARLA: *(Giving him the look)* Ain't that the truth.

(A beat, as LEO *catches up with the insult)*

CARLA: Man, what was I thinking? I was not ready for this.

LEO: The slime, you mean? It is pretty deep around here sometimes.

CARLA: No, I did six years in sales, I know about slime. It's the lies. Naked, buff, big, fat, flesh-shaking lies.

LEO: So the business world is any better?

CARLA: At least business has a code of honor. "Keep your hands on your wallet, babe, 'cause if you turn your back, I can pick your pocket." Up here, it's "My fellow Americans, I will now pick your pocket while I'm staring you in the face and swearing that I'm not—*and* I'll take your pants and your jock strap while I'm at it."

LEO: "But I'm doing it to save you."

CARLA: Right. "From the terrorists."

LEO: Or "the Other Party. And it's costing you billions."

CARLA: "And you should re-elect me so I can do it to you some more!" *(A beat; she is softening here)* We must all be out of our minds. Maybe it's something in the food supply...O K, I'm stumped, I admit it. I do not know how to fix this. Any suggestions, Speechwriter, while this campaign still has a pulse?

LEO: Here. *(He offers her the speech)*

CARLA: *(Taking it)* This better not have the word redistricting in it.

LEO: It's not about policy. Or even personal attack.

CARLA: So what's left?

LEO: Ideals.

CARLA: You want him to waste a whole speech on ideals?

LEO: If his words are bigger, he will be, too.

CARLA: A beard, no necktie and ideals. That's your suggestion?

LEO: At least give it a try. What have you got to lose?

CARLA: Besides my reputation and my job? Don't get your hopes up. *(Thumbing through the text)* I wonder how much money we'd save if we just concede now? *(Looking up, finding him still there)* Would you go find something useful to do?

(He exits. Lights. Transition)

Scene Six

(Lobby of the downtown Washington, DC, office building where FRANCIS works. It is night. FRANCIS, in custodial uniform, works an electric buffer machine)

FRANCIS: "The world has never had a good definition of the word liberty, and the American people, just now, are in much want of one. We all declare for liberty; in using the same word, we do not all mean the same thing. With some, the word liberty may mean for each man to do as he pleases with himself and the product of his labor; while with others the word may mean for men to do as they please with other men, and the product of other men's labor. Each of these things is called by two different and incompatible names— liberty and tyranny."

(Enter somewhat cautiously a lawyer-type, middle-aged, with the requisite briefcase and conservative suit. This is HAROLD DALY, lawyer-lobbyist-image shaper. He may have been eavesdropping)

DALY: Hey.

(FRANCIS *halts the machine, freezes*)

DALY: Doing a heck of a job on that floor. You can see your face in it.

(A beat. FRANCIS *restarts the machine, continues buffing, avoiding eye contact with the man.)*

DALY: You're new here. Aren't you? In the building? ...You know, you remind me of someone. I don't suppose we've met before?

(FRANCIS *shuts off the machine. A beat*)

FRANCIS: No.

DALY: Lobby's never looked better. *(An introduction)* Hoffman, Sanders, Daly. Fifth and sixth floors. I'm Daly.

FRANCIS: Harold Daly. The papers call you "the king of the king-makers."

DALY: Among other things. What's your name?

FRANCIS: I, sir, am... *(This takes an effort)* I'm Francis.

DALY: Francis. They've got you on the night shift.

FRANCIS: Yes.

DALY: You and I might be the only workers left in the building at this hour.

FRANCIS: I prefer it. The quiet.

DALY: You know something? I do, too. I think I'm becoming more of a loner as I get older.

FRANCIS: Contemplation befits the later years.

DALY: *(A beat)* Would you say that again for me?

FRANCIS: "Contemplation befits the later years."

DALY: I thought that's what I heard. Francis. Mind if I run something by you? Get your opinion. My firm does lobbying, public opinion research—among other things. We lawyers get bogged down in detail, lose the big picture. I find it helpful to hear from the man in the street, so to speak.

FRANCIS: *(Being witty)* Or the buffer in the lobby.

DALY: *(Appreciating it)* That's right. So here's the issue. Let's see what you think. Excessive pay for corporate execs. You know, multiple millions in salary, sweetheart stock deals, etc. Let's say you're a congressman—in fact, you're one of my boys. You take a huge amount of money from these overpaid execs. But polls show that voters overwhelmingly think it's bad. So your take on it is, it's bad. *(Quickly here, the salesman with a pitch)* But. Over-compensated C E Os actually project a positive corporate image of prosperity and healthy cash reserves, so overcompensation is a sort of controlled excess that encourages a free-market economy, reinforces the vital infrastructure of American democracy and gives the nation's kids something to shoot for, what do you think?

FRANCIS: Labyrinthine.

DALY: Say again?

FRANCIS: Excessive pay is bad because it is wrong. The matter is simple. Complicating it is dishonest. For the orator, the last, best hope of persuasion lies in the simple.

DALY: *(Searching for a pen)* Could you...? Do you min if I jot that down? "The last, best hope of persuasion..." That's good. What do you think people want, Francis? In general. Off the top of your head.

FRANCIS: Inspiration.

DALY: Not money? Security? Health insurance?

FRANCIS: Temporal and corporal satisfaction are never equal to satisfaction of the spirit.

DALY: Right... It's funny you say that. I heard a speech the other night. Congressman. Guy named Carpenter. He's running against our client. I have to admit, it was actually inspiring. Never heard anything like it.

FRANCIS: Yes you have.

DALY: It gave me a shiver. How many speeches by a politician these days give you a shiver?

FRANCIS: Precious few.

DALY: And this guy Carpenter is such a loser. My job is to break him down into bite-size chunks, chew him up and spit out the bones. You follow politics?

FRANCIS: Some.

DALY: We've got his bank records, medical records, college transcripts, family history—there's a disgraceful embarrassment in there somewhere. Has to be. Rules of the game.

FRANCIS: You sound worried, Mister Daly.

DALY: Do I? Have you always been a floor buffer, Francis?

FRANCIS: No.

DALY: No, I didn't think so. Where'd you go to school?

FRANCIS: I had little formal education.

DALY: Self-taught?

FRANCIS: Largely. I attended a one-room schoolhouse as a child.

DALY: Seriously?

FRANCIS: Oh yes.

DALY: I didn't think they had those anymore. How did you wind up polishing the floor in my lobby?

FRANCIS: I suffered a disappointment.

DALY: Really.

FRANCIS: Yes.

DALY: Tell me about it.

FRANCIS: I can't.

DALY: *(A beat; respectfully)* Francis? Can I try that thing? *(The buffer)*

FRANCIS: This?

DALY: Yeah.

FRANCIS: Here. Stand firm. Let the machine do the work all around you.

(DALY turns on the machine, buffs happily for a moment.)

DALY: Look at that shine... This is the most useful thing I've done all day... Manual labor. Frees up your mind.

FRANCIS: Yes.

DALY: At home I used to mow. Same kind of thing. Loved it. But my wife hired landscapers. Said she was worried about my heart. But she wasn't.

FRANCIS: No?

DALY: No. Pure malice. She saw I enjoyed it. So she took it away. She's a very unhappy person.

FRANCIS: I am sorry to learn it.

DALY: Yeah.

FRANCIS: What is the cause of your wife's unhappiness?

DALY: Me.

FRANCIS: Then might you not also be the remedy?

DALY: *(He thinks about that.)* We're probably beyond remedies. You know why I stay late at the office most nights, Francis?

FRANCIS: No.

DALY: I don't want to go home. *(He stops the machine.)* I don't love my wife anymore. I haven't loved her for ten years. I don't have the courage to say it to her.

FRANCIS: I suspect, sir, that you say it every evening with your late arrival home.

DALY: Why doesn't she answer me, then?

FRANCIS: Perhaps she does so—with her malice, as you put it.

DALY: We've stayed together mostly because of the girls, but they're both married now, so what's the point anymore? We've wounded each other so many times. Scars on top of scars.

FRANCIS: Two armies aligned against one another. One side charges, the other falls back, then counters. No decisive blow is struck, so the battle continues endlessly, until fighting becomes its own excuse for more fighting.

DALY: So how do we stop?

FRANCIS: The greater courage now is in diplomacy.

DALY: No, we've talked and talked. It always turns into an argument. Sometimes I think about just packing it all up and going away. Did you ever feel that way?

FRANCIS: There's abundant land in the western territories.

DALY: Just jump in the car and drive till I come to a place that looks like where I'd want to start over.

FRANCIS: Springfield, Illinois.

DALY: I'd look for some place small and quiet. Where a man can cut his own damn grass.

FRANCIS: Invite your spouse to go with you.

DALY: What? No. She'll be glad to see me go.

FRANCIS: Allow yourself the opportunity to be surprised.

DALY: *(He ponders that a moment. Sadly)* You know, Francis, I got more pleasure out of shining this floor than anything I've done in a month.

FRANCIS: What if you were to say to her, I wish to love you as fully as I once did. And ask her if she too does not wish to love as fully.

DALY: She'll laugh at me. She'll think I've gone crazy.

FRANCIS: Go crazy, Mister Daly. In a city so desperately sane, crazy is the remedy.

DALY: Francis. Call me Harry.

FRANCIS: Harry. Call me— *(He has to think about this a beat.)* Would you be willing to call me Abe?

DALY: "Abe"?

FRANCIS: Just for tonight. If you have no objection.

DALY: Abe it is. Will you do me a favor, Abe? I'd like the pleasure of buying you a drink.

FRANCIS: I am forbidden to drink. And I have work still to do.

DALY: I own this building. And I say you've done enough work on it for tonight.

(Lights. Transition)

Scene Seven.

(LEO and CARLA in a Capitol Hill lounge. It is late evening of a long work day. They are reading early editions of the next day's newspapers to one another: first reviews of the "new Dave")

CARLA: Look at this. Look. "The whole level of this previously mean-spirited campaign has now been raised up by a series of visionary and frankly inspiring speeches from a career politician many thought boring and unremarkable."

LEO: "Is there still a place in American politics for an intelligent and inspiring dialogue with voters? Dave Carpenter thinks so, and judging by the standing ovation the unshaven and open-collared veteran received from a packed meeting hall last week, voters agree."

CARLA: It's working.

LEO: It's actually working!

(Carried away by the euphoria of the moment, he throws his arms around CARLA and hugs her—freezes when he realizes the impropriety of his action—then instantly disengages. Embarrassed, he does his best to ignore what has just occurred.)

LEO: It's working.

CARLA: I am officially amazed, all right? And I know nothing about writing speeches. *You* know about speech writing.

LEO: Me? I wrote those snoozers on redistricting.

CARLA: But this time you got it right.

LEO: I got lucky. I hit on a couple of phrases that worked.

CARLA: Come off it, Leo. There's more to it than that.

LEO: So you know.

CARLA: Damn right I know. Leo. You moved an audience to get up on its feet and cheer. That is a serious gift.

LEO: It wasn't me, Carla. *(A beat; pause for the ethical dilemma... and the unethical bail out)* It was Dave.

CARLA: Oh, stop. "It was Dave." Who's in charge up here, really? Of the four hundred-and-whatever elected reps who park their asses in those Congressional seats, how many of them think for themselves? Or actually think, period?

LEO: A dozen, maybe.

CARLA: A dozen, maybe. The rest have staff like us who tell them *how* to say what the opinion polls tell them they *should* say, and we all follow the money that tells them what they *can* say. But nobody, absolutely nobody, talks from the heart to the heart about integrity and principles and risking everything for what you believe in. You did that. Dave didn't do that.

LEO: It was just a speech.

CARLA: You know what that speech was? It was Lincolnesque.

LEO: Carla—

CARLA: No. That's why people come to Washington, to hear words like that.

LEO: You're a closet idealist!

(She laughs, or scoffs.)

LEO: Under that tough-as-nails, chief-of-staff veneer, you're really just a, just a...

CARLA: A tough-as-nails chief of staff.

LEO: Oh.

CARLA: I've been called a lot of things, but "idealist" isn't on the list.

LEO: Right.

CARLA: You see what they do to dreamers around here. Look at you.

LEO: Me?

CARLA: "Whatever it takes." That's my motto. If I can use ideals to get Dave Carpenter re-elected, great. Dish 'em up.

LEO: *(A beat, as he weighs the risk)* I don't believe you.

CARLA: Believe me.

LEO: *(The newspaper)* Look what that speech did. You said it was good. It touched something, inside you.

CARLA: That makes me an idealist?

LEO: You could be pulling down corporate money somewhere. But you chose this. There's an ideal hiding inside you.

CARLA: O K. And here it is: a high-profile job in Washington builds name recognition and power contacts, which means a salary bump when you go back to corporate.

LEO: You're doing it for the money?

CARLA: Sweetheart, money *is* an ideal to most people.

LEO: Money. That's easy for you. But ideals—those are hard. From the heart, to the heart. Risking everything.

That's really why you're up here. You just don't dare
admit it.

(A beat; was that a little too accurate for comfort?)

CARLA: Don't project your fantasies on me.

LEO: I think you're scared.

CARLA: Hey. If I was scared, you think I'd admit it to
you?

LEO: Right. I'm your subordinate.

CARLA: And I'm your boss. Don't forget it, if you want
to stay employed.

LEO: You don't need to do that with me, Carla. I'm not
competing with you.

CARLA: Why the hell not? What's the matter with you?
Stand up to me when I talk to you like that! Don't you
have any—damn—ambition?

LEO: Yes.

CARLA: You can write a speech like that and you're
working this stupid little job? You're not even in charge
of anyone! How do you expect me to be attracted to
you if you're so goddamn pathetic?

LEO: How do I expect you to what?

CARLA: And get yourself some treatment for that
speech problem, for God's sake! You better figure
out pretty soon what it is you want out of life, mister,
because you're not getting any younger and prettier.

LEO: What I want—?

CARLA: Yeah.

LEO: Inspiration. The same as you.

CARLA: Well, what inspires me right now is winning
this election. I want Dave's poll numbers analyzed, top

to bottom, inside-out, focus groups, surveys, figure out how to react—

LEO: Carla. Fuck Dave's numbers.

CARLA: What did you just say?

LEO: He's just a politician. Sooner or later they'll replace him with another one, just as dull and mediocre.

CARLA: So? That's called American democracy.

LEO: Don't you get it? This is our chance to change the rules. We might even change national politics. Vision. Inspiration. A dialogue. Not "please, please re-elect me" and not "my opponent is a serial liar." That's what's happening here. We can make a real, actual, honest-to-God difference. We turn conventional Washington upside down. We kick it in the ass. Whether we win or not doesn't matter.

CARLA: Whoa, whoa.

LEO: Didn't you ever want to break the rules when you were a kid, just for the pure joy of breaking something sacred? Or just to see the look on the faces of the rule-makers? If we're going to lose this thing, let's lose gloriously. Let's jump from the tallest building and go out with a splat. Throw out everything we think we know. Numbers, polls, party platforms, everything. This is a once-in-a-lifetime opportunity, Carla. Take it with me.

(A beat. She's staring at him, thinking hard about this)

CARLA: Leo.

LEO: What.

CARLA: We're getting out of here.

LEO: Where?

CARLA: You will walk back to my apartment with me. Then you will come up and have a drink.

LEO: That sounds like an order.

CARLA: So obey it.

(They prepare to go. Enter FRANCIS. LEO *doesn't see him at first.)*

FRANCIS: Good evening, Leo.

LEO: *(Turns to see him. Speechless a moment)* Francis?

CARLA: *(To* LEO*)* Who is this? Is this your brother?

LEO: *(Ignoring her)* What are you doing here?

FRANCIS: Mister Daly invited me for a drink.

LEO: *Harold* Daly?

CARLA: *The* Harold Daly?

LEO: You're having a drink with Harold Daly?

FRANCIS: Just a small one. I am forbidden to drink.

LEO: But how did you—?

FRANCIS: He works in the building I clean.

CARLA: You clean Harold Daly's building?

LEO: You're supposed to go directly home after work.

FRANCIS: He insisted. We are in the dining section. Would you both care to join us?

CARLA: Yes!

LEO: No!

CARLA: *(Butting in)* I'm Carla Rourke, your brother's boss. I know who you are.

FRANCIS: Thank you, Miss Rourke. For some reason, most people don't recognize me. It may be the uniform.

LEO: Francis, we're leaving. Come on.

FRANCIS: I don't wish to leave.

LEO: Francis.

FRANCIS: Harry would be insulted.

CARLA: You call him "Harry"?

LEO: Francis. Now.

CARLA: Don't tug at him like that, Leo.

LEO: Stay out of this. *(Pulling him aside, trying to keep his voice down)* You're on medication, you're not supposed to go *near* alcohol.

FRANCIS: You've forgotten. I am better now. I have ceased to take the medicine.

LEO: No, you haven't.

FRANCIS: But I have.

LEO: No. I've been giving it to you.

FRANCIS: Leo, what are you...?

LEO: I mix it in your food.

FRANCIS: No, Leo.

LEO: I didn't think it was safe to tell you.

CARLA: You gave him medicine and didn't tell him?

LEO: *(Ignoring her)* The medicine is meant to help you, Francis.

(A beat...and FRANCIS brings his fist down violently on their table)

FRANCIS: *(Furious, but still controlled)* Now are we engaged in a great civil war. There are traitors and rebels in the capital, Miss Rourke, did you know that?

LEO: Not here, Francis. I mean it.

FRANCIS: Spies and betrayers!

LEO: Francis.

(LEO takes his arm, but FRANCIS frees himself with a violent gesture that almost knocks his brother over.)

FRANCIS: *(Loudly, for the whole establishment)* Where does this assembly stand on emancipation of the Negro!?

LEO: Francis, don't.

FRANCIS: Speak up! Your president addresses you! "I do not say that the Negro is equal to the white man. But I do say that he has an equal right to live in freedom!"

LEO: They're going to call the police, Francis.

FRANCIS: "In giving freedom to the slave, we assure freedom to the free!"

LEO: *(To the bar patrons)* We're leaving, people. He's had too much to drink.

FRANCIS: "The world will little note, nor long remember what we say here!"

LEO: Let's hope so.

FRANCIS: But it can never forget what Leo did here!

LEO: Francis, come on.

CARLA: Mister President!

(That surprises and freezes FRANCIS. *A beat, as he and* CARLA *look at one another: Is she friend or foe?)*

CARLA: Please, sir. It's time to get you back to the White House. Your cabinet is meeting. We will escort you, sir. If you agree.

(A beat...and FRANCIS *exits, left. At a look from* LEO*)*

CARLA: I know what I'm doing. Go!

(She pushes him toward the exit, left, and they both hurry after Francis)

(Lights. Transition)

Scene Eight

(LEO's apartment, a couple of hours later. CARLA, pacing, but quietly, more reserved. Enter LEO.)

CARLA: Is he asleep now?

LEO: I think so. Finally.

CARLA: There's no coffee. Nothing in the refrigerator. Or the cupboards. Or the whole apartment. *(A beat)* Does he do this a lot, flip-out in public like that?

LEO: If he would just take his damn medication...

CARLA: So. Let's hear it.

LEO: What.

CARLA: The whole story.

LEO: The story is, I have a brother who's psychotic. All right? End of story.

CARLA: Maybe you want to talk about it.

LEO: And maybe I don't.

CARLA: It'll help, Leo, trust me. So he was a genius. Big deal. There are hundreds of geniuses out there.

LEO: Not like Francis. On strategy, he was like a chess master, he could see five, six, seven moves ahead. Nobody could out-debate him. He made points like a boxer, pow, pow, pow, argument over. He had no patience with people who were dumber and slower, and everybody was dumber and slower than Francis. Sooner or later, he'd alienate even the people who liked him, and he wasn't easy to like. He was relentless. He had these impossible standards, nobody could live up to them.

CARLA: Including him.

LEO: After the breakdown no one from his staff came to the hospital. They blamed him for going mad, like he committed a crime. He was the warning that nobody wanted to hear. Me especially.

CARLA: Stop beating yourself up.

LEO: I'm quitting the campaign.

CARLA: The hell you are.

LEO: I need to spend more time with Francis.

CARLA: Why?

LEO: "Why"? Look at him.

CARLA: He functions. He's got a job. He even chums around with Harold Daly.

LEO: He's psychotic. He thinks he's the reappearance of a legendary historic figure.

CARLA: Leo. You just described half the politicians in Washington.

LEO: I should have taken him away months ago.

CARLA: But you didn't.

LEO: I was scared. *You* try to start over someplace new with a madman brother. If things fall apart...

CARLA: Leo.

LEO: Madness runs in families, you know.

CARLA: Enough with the self-pity. You are a man who writes electrifying speeches.

LEO: They're not that electrifying.

(She begins to advance on him; he retreats.)

CARLA: Back there in that bar you talked about changing national politics, turning this city on its head. There was fire in your eyes. And I bought it. I was inspired, Leo. By you.

LEO: You were?

CARLA: Pumped. You don't know your own talents.

LEO: No, I do know.

CARLA: This election is in *your* hands. You can do this. *(Here she begins to undress him: glasses first, then shirt, shoes....)* There is a strong, capable man in there somewhere and I'm going to let you prove it to me. It's time you had a little motivational meeting with the boss.

LEO: What, here?

CARLA: I said, whatever it takes, and I meant it. Leo. What's going through your mind right now?

LEO: An escape plan.

CARLA: Forget it. There is no escape. What's going through your mind is, you're alone, late at night, with an attractive available woman.

(The belt...)

LEO: Who is also my boss.

CARLA: So follow instructions. It's time for your performance review.

LEO: I request a postponement.

(The pants...)

CARLA: Denied. You're trembling. Be honest with me. How long?

LEO: I don't know, I never— Average?

CARLA: No, how long since you had sex?

LEO: Oh. A while. You know, a couple of...

CARLA: Weeks?

LEO: Years?

CARLA: *(Turning him toward his bedroom, giving him a shove)* March. *(As he goes)* This city is more destructive than I thought.

(He exits, left, she follows. After a beat, FRANCIS *emerges, right, silently, on tip-toe and listens discreetly for sounds coming from his brother's bedroom)*

FRANCIS: *(Cheerfully)* "We say we are for the Union. The world will not forget that we say this. We know how to save the Union. The world knows we do know how to save it. We hold the power and bear the responsibility. In giving freedom to the slave, we assure freedom to the free—honorable alike in what we give, and what we preserve..." *(A beat, as he listens again.)*
    "The way is plain, generous, just—a way the world will forever applaud, and God must forever bless."

*(*CARLA, *in bathrobe, emerges from the bedroom; her hair is in wild disarray, she appears to be almost in shock. She staggers past* FRANCIS, *not acknowledging him.)*

CARLA: Whoa. It really *was* years.

(She exits.)

*(*LEO *emerges, in boxers and tee shirt. He and* FRANCIS *exchange looks.)*

(Lights)

END OF ACT ONE

ACT TWO

Scene One

(Back in the office, a week later. CARLA, *in a temper;* LEO, *in despair)*

LEO: So where were we?

CARLA: Stuck. Read it again.

LEO: Which one?

CARLA: The original Lincoln.

LEO: *(Reading from his papers)* It's from his annual message to Congress, 1863.

CARLA: Who cares where it's from!? Just go.

LEO: "The dogmas of the quiet past are inadequate to the stormy present."

CARLA: O K. So?

LEO: O K. So something like: We are now in a storm, ladies and gentlemen. A raging storm of the present. And if we think we can just take a dogma of the quiet past—

CARLA: No. If we think we can *use* a dogma—

LEO: No. If *they* think—

CARLA: If *they* think they can *use* a dogma of the quiet past—

LEO: Then the raging storms of the present—

CARLA: The raging storms of the present will soak—

LEO: They will flood, they will devastate—

CARLA: They will break the levees!

LEO: The raging storms of the present will break the levees—

CARLA: And rip the roofs off the dogmas of the quiet past.

(A beat. They stare at one another. Maybe they have something....)

LEO: And cause heavy damage—

CARLA: Irreparable heavy damage—

LEO: The raging storms of the present will cause irreparable heavy damage—

CARLA: To the furniture of the future—

LEO: Inside the houses—

CARLA: The roofless houses of the present! *(A beat)* God, that sucks. What is wrong with you?

LEO: "Me"? And what is a "dogma of the quiet past" anyway?

CARLA: How should I know? Wait! *(She's got it!)* You can't teach an old dogma new tricks.

LEO: What?

CARLA: No, put that down. That's good.

LEO: It is not good.

CARLA: Well, come up with something better, then!

LEO: I'm trying! Why don't *you* contribute something besides criticism?

CARLA: We have been at this three days and we have maybe four lines.

LEO: Six lines.

CARLA: Why is it taking so long?

LEO: It's hard, that's why.

CARLA: Well, how did you do the other ones?

LEO: I don't know, inspiration.

CARLA: If we don't pull this off, you're out of a job. That's not inspiring enough?

(A beat)

LEO: Carla. The other night...

CARLA: I don't want to talk about it.

LEO: It was the most incredible—

CARLA: Just write the damn speech, dammit! That was the whole point, remember? Network coverage, Leo, thirty-four hours and fifteen minutes from now. But we need a speech! Try another one.

LEO: *(Finding one)* It's from the same address to Congress.

CARLA: Just—! Read it!

LEO: "The fiery trial through which we pass will light us down, in honor or dishonor, to the latest generation."

CARLA: All right. So. A trial.

LEO: We're going through a fiery trial, ladies and gentlemen. A long, exhausting fiery trial.

CARLA: By a jury of our peers.

LEO: No. By fire.

CARLA: A long, exhausting trial by fire by a jury of our peers.

LEO: There's nothing in there about a jury.

CARLA: That's anti-democratic.

LEO: *(Yelling)* It's about fire! A trial by fire!

CARLA: Don't you yell at me. *(Yelling)* Don't you *ever* yell at me! *(A beat)* The trial by fire—

LEO: That we are undergoing—

CARLA: That we must endure—

LEO: All must endure—

CARLA: The long, exhausting trial by fire that we all must endure—

LEO: Will burn...? Will light...?

CARLA: Will light up our lives.

LEO: What?

CARLA: With democracy.

LEO: What?

CARLA: For generations, in honor or dishonor, despite the dogma of the raging storms of the present that rip the roofs off the, off the, off the quiet past.

(A beat. She stares at him: I dare you.)

LEO: O K. That's good.

CARLA: It's garbage.

LEO: No.

CARLA: It's trash. I've had it.

LEO: Dave has to have this speech tonight.

CARLA: Do you realize what we're doing here? We are plundering Lincoln's grave!

LEO: We are borrowing from his legacy.

CARLA: We're plagiarizing!

LEO: We are not. It's copyright unencumbered!

CARLA: *(Finally losing it)* Oh, this is so stupid!! All this for Congressman! Dave! Carpenter!? That spineless human vacuum!? How did he ever get elected the first time?

LEO: He lied.

CARLA: Of course he lied!

LEO: *(Tentatively, cautious of her anger)* He told the voters he had an actual brain.

CARLA: How could they fall for that!? I mean, look at the evidence. If they ever get a court order to open up his skull...

LEO: Medical miracle. *(Headlines)* "Brainless Man Elected to Congress." "Colleagues Sympathetic. It Could Happen to Any of Us, Say Senators."

(A beat, as they look at one another. Does this mean they can be friends again?)

LEO: Carla. The other night was so...

CARLA: Just finish the speech! How could you suddenly go from spinning gold to taking all week to sweat out six bad lines?

LEO: I just need a little help.

CARLA: You want help robbing Lincoln, why don't you go ask Francis? Your brother's the mad genius who thinks he's— *(She stares at him; comes the light.)* Who thinks he's...Leo.

LEO: I was going to tell you.

CARLA: Francis wrote the speeches.

LEO: That's not true, completely. He gave me the best phrases. I filled in. It was his idea.

CARLA: I went to bed with the wrong brother.

LEO: How could I tell you? Or Dave? A former mental patient for a speechwriter?

CARLA: How low can you crawl?

LEO: O K, I made a bad judgment. But it's over. I won't sacrifice Francis again.

(As she exits)

LEO: Carla, wait. The deadline! We're only five points down!

(She's gone.)

LEO: O K, fine, I can write it myself!! *(A beat; he reads the next Lincoln phrase from his papers.)* "We shall nobly win or meanly lose the last best hope of earth." Right. God. How did he *do* that?

(Lights. Transition)

Scene Two

(A city park. DALY *and* FRANCIS *in conversation)*

DALY: And then, Francis, then after that—I couldn't believe it. Can I tell you this? This is so unlike me. I never talk about my private life.

FRANCIS: Tell me.

DALY: She just...melted. And then so did I. Tears, everything. It was incredible. We jumped into each other's arms. Right there on the hundred thousand dollar Persian carpet in the master dining room, like newlyweds, we just— I was, I got so— And *she*, she just— We both, I mean— It must have been ten years since, you know, with such passion...

FRANCIS: I share in your joy.

DALY: Ten years. I filled them with nothing but work, Francis. And now they're gone.

FRANCIS: Better to embrace the years to come than regret the years departed.

DALY: I feel like my life has changed. All of a sudden I feel, I don't know...

FRANCIS: Emancipated.

DALY: That's it exactly.

FRANCIS: The war has had so few victories that we rejoice all the more at the present triumph.

DALY: I don't always understand you, Francis. But I always feel you're worth listening to.

FRANCIS: A man wishes above all to be heard. For that I thank you, Harry.

DALY: No, I should thank you—for rescuing my marriage. *(A beat)* So you're not married, yourself.

FRANCIS: No.

DALY: You live alone?

FRANCIS: I live with my brother.

DALY: And what's he do?

FRANCIS: He is involved in politics.

DALY: Aren't we all. Who's he work for?

FRANCIS: Harry, forgive me, but... Could we change the subject?

DALY: Sure, O K. So Francis, look. We carry a lot of highly paid consultants on our payroll. Half of 'em are a bunch of hopeless old farts who couldn't tell you which way the wind was blowing if they stood in a gale in their underpants. What do you make as a custodian?

FRANCIS: I don't recall, precisely.

DALY: Let's say we double it. And you report directly to me.

FRANCIS: But what would I be expected to do?

DALY: Talk to me.

FRANCIS: On what topic?

DALY: People, politics. Truth, beauty, exit polls. Whatever comes up.

FRANCIS: I don't know, Harry.

DALY: What's there to know? It's what we do now, you just make a little money at it, that's all. Difference is, maybe a couple of your phrases make it into a speech or two here or there.

FRANCIS: No! I mean— I feel uneasy about it.

LEO: My client needs something to fire back at this Carpenter guy, Francis, and I think you're just the man.

FRANCIS: I'm not, Harry, believe me, I'm not. I have to decline.

DALY: Sure, O K. *(A beat)* You know, Francis, anybody else in this town would jump.

FRANCIS: I apologize.

DALY: No, don't. I admire you for it.

(Exit DALY...FRANCIS *remains alone for a long moment, deep in thought, seated in his Lincoln Memorial pose... Then he addresses the Congress.)*

FRANCIS: "With malice toward none; with charity for all; with firmness in the right, as God gave us to see the right, let us strive on to finish the work we are in; to bind up the nation's wounds; to care for him who shall have borne the battle, and for his widow, and his orphan—to do all which may achieve and cherish a just and lasting peace, among ourselves, and with all nations."

(*Enter* SECRETARY OF WAR.)

SECRETARY OF WAR: I used to give talks like that once. Did I tell you?

FRANCIS: You did, Edwin.

SECRETARY OF WAR: I was a G S-14. I had my own office. Not one of these piddly little cubicles. An office, with a door. Big enough for a plant, large potted plant.

FRANCIS: You were a man of accomplishment, Edwin.

SECRETARY OF WAR: I had a staff of six. Or seven. I was a G S-15. I made decisions left and right. Millions of dollars flowed through my hands, Abe. I had direct access to classified documents. I knew things. Shocking things. I carried them around up here, day and night. But people got nervous, they got jealous. The big-ass, bigwig muckety-mucks, that's who did me in. And my wife, Abe—soon as they started coming after me, she got scared, filed for divorce, and poof! Gone. Took my son right out from under me. Sold the house, sold the car. Left me defenseless.

FRANCIS: Edwin. You will stay with me tonight.

SECRETARY OF WAR: (*Surveying the city*) You know what we have here, Abe? Monuments. Monuments on every damn corner. Dead soldiers, dead presidents, dead politicians. This is a city of the dead, Abe. That's what we've created here. Look at you. You've been dead, what? Hundred and fifty years? We're a lot like the Incas. We even have the temples with the long stone steps. Human sacrifice. Happens here every day.

FRANCIS: You're feeling melancholy this evening.

SECRETARY OF WAR: I always feel down at Christmas.

FRANCIS: It is October, Edwin.

SECRETARY OF WAR: Yeah, well. They cancel my government life insurance at the end of the year. It'll pay for Danny's whole college education, start to finish.

FRANCIS: It pains me to hear you speak like that.

SECRETARY OF WAR: It pains *me*, Abe, to be alive. What pills do you take for that?

(Exit the SECRETARY OF WAR. FRANCIS *watches him go, then settles sadly into his Lincoln Memorial pose. Lights down on* FRANCIS *as* LEO *enters, looking like a man who's been up all night beating his head against a wall.)*

LEO: She had to be gentle—I insisted on that—no forcing him, no threats, nothing to set him off. And my name stays out of it, it was her idea. If we win, then everything is forgiven. Winner-take-all. That's how it works. Betrayal. Sacrifice. Human flesh. Rules of the game.

*(*LEO *watches* CARLA *enter. They exchange glances. He exits. Lights back up on* FRANCIS, *seated presidentially on his park bench.)*

CARLA: Hello, Francis.

FRANCIS: Miss Rourke? I am surprised to see you here at the White House. How did you get past my security man?

CARLA: There isn't any security man.

FRANCIS: That's alarming. I shall have to speak to him when he returns. Won't you sit down? *(She sits.)* Have you come to petition your government?

CARLA: No.

FRANCIS: In a great democracy, a president is accessible to his constituents. Even in times of war. Perhaps especially in times of war.

CARLA: Francis.

FRANCIS: You may address me as Mister President.

CARLA: I can see right through you.

(A beat)

FRANCIS: I hope for your sake, Miss Rourke, you are in no way aligned with the rebels. I don't wish to have you arrested.

CARLA: You know what I'm talking about.

FRANCIS: So. You're a Douglas Democrat. Opposed to every move I make. I can tell you this: no one is more opposed to the war than I.

CARLA: Francis.

FRANCIS: But it has been thrust upon us. We have no choice but to fight on to the end.

CARLA: You wrote the speeches.

FRANCIS: I have malice toward none—

CARLA: Leo told me.

FRANCIS: Charity for all.

CARLA: And you are no more insane than the rest of us.

FRANCIS: *(A beat. Controlled anger)* Oh, faint praise. *(A return to character)* Why are you here in my office?

CARLA: You're sitting on a park bench that's covered in bird shit.

FRANCIS: No. *You* may be sitting on a park bench covered in whatever you like. I am in the oval office.

CARLA: Here. *(She smears a touch of bird shit on him.)* What do you call that?

FRANCIS: How dare you. I can have you shot as a spy.

CARLA: Go ahead. Call in your soldiers.

FRANCIS: No. *(A beat; presidentially)* They are busy defending the Union. I bid you good day.

(He starts to leave, she stops him.)

CARLA: You can't fool me the way you fool Leo.

FRANCIS: I find you incomprehensible, madam.

(Again, she stops him from leaving.)

CARLA: You don't think you're Abraham Lincoln. Or Lincoln's ghost, or his reincarnation or anything else. It's all an act.

FRANCIS: So. You *are* a rebel.

CARLA: I know some things about crazy, Francis—more than I wish. My ex-husband had a real breakdown, five years ago this Christmas. Bipolar with schizoaffective symptoms, very ugly. It was in his family, but he didn't tell me that when I married him. We went through the whole treatment torture—therapy, drugs, hospitals. But he wasn't getting better, and it was killing me. So I had him committed.

FRANCIS: I pity you, madam. But I have a country to run.

CARLA: Why pretend to be Lincoln, Francis? I mean, when you get right down to it, he was a liar and a dictator.

FRANCIS: What?

CARLA: And a racist.

FRANCIS: He was the best this country ever produced!

CARLA: "He" was?

FRANCIS: I was. I am.

CARLA: Aren't you confused, Francis?

FRANCIS: You are confused! And a traitor!

CARLA: Habeas corpus.

FRANCIS: We are at war.

CARLA: He suspended the most basic rule of civil liberty, without a vote in Congress—

FRANCIS: So that I could secure the Union.

CARLA: So that he could rule like a dictator. Thousands of innocent Americans thrown into jail without trial, held indefinitely.

FRANCIS: Rebel sympathizers and spies.

CARLA: Anyone he suspected. Anyone he didn't trust.

FRANCIS: I am and will always be the Great Emancipator.

CARLA: Emancipate the slaves right back to Africa. That was the plan: reverse-colonization. Ship 'em out, problem solved.

FRANCIS: It was only a proposal.

CARLA: With a budget and a timetable, estimated number of ships, a country in Africa all picked out.

FRANCIS: It was to be voluntary—

CARLA: Oh, we know all about "voluntary". The truth is, he never thought blacks were equal to whites—

FRANCIS: Slavery is wrong, it must be destroyed—

CARLA: Not mentally, not morally—

FRANCIS: That was the central idea—

CARLA: Indians he treated even worse—

FRANCIS: That was the heart of the matter—

CARLA: He let the South be burned to the ground at the end—

FRANCIS: The rebellion had to be crushed—

CARLA: It was revenge. Ethnic cleansing.

FRANCIS: Stop it—

CARLA: There are no heroes, Francis. Lincoln was a politician, a liar like the rest of them—

FRANCIS: Stop it!

CARLA: Like Dave Carpenter—

FRANCIS: No! Damn you!!

(He grabs her as if he would like to smash her. She is defiant, unafraid.)

CARLA: There's the old Francis. Welcome back.

(He lets her go. He has lost this round.)

FRANCIS: What is it you want from me?

CARLA: I want you to write one more speech.

(A beat, as he figures it out)

FRANCIS: So. If I am insane, it is cruel of you to demand another speech. But if I am as normal as you...it's only politics.

CARLA: Why this little vaudeville act of yours, Francis? What's the point?

FRANCIS: The war. Look at the carnage all around you. Good people. Worthy ideas. Cut down, sliced apart, blown to pieces. The butchery of honor, integrity, faith. Aren't you repulsed by it?

CARLA: *(Skeptical)* That's what you're hiding from?

FRANCIS: I came here a dozen years ago, a common soldier. I failed to make any headway against the enemy. Worse, I contributed to our own losses. So I withdrew me from the field.

CARLA: You know who you are and where you are. Do you deny it?

FRANCIS: No.

CARLA: You know the day, the year. You know who the president is—the current one.

FRANCIS: Alas, yes.

CARLA: And you know how to use Lincoln—how to update his best phrases so they sound fresh.

FRANCIS: They have never gone stale.

CARLA: You even know how to make Dave Carpenter stop sounding like the hopeless embarrassment he really is.

FRANCIS: Correct.

CARLA: Then you're sane. You just proved it. What you're doing now—it's a strategy, a conscious choice. You *choose* to play Lincoln.

FRANCIS: Or Lincoln chooses to play me.

CARLA: What is that supposed to mean?

FRANCIS: Who knows what happens to the spirits of great men when they die? Do you imagine they simply vanish from the world, and all is done? What if they seek to return one day and inhabit some humble vessel, such as myself? What if the city is full of such spirits, even now, searching in vain to return?

CARLA: Get serious, Francis.

FRANCIS: Oh, you will dismiss it. You will mock the possibility because it is not *normal*. Everyone here is terrified of the not-normal. The slightest deviation is a threat to national security.

CARLA: Francis, look—

FRANCIS: Courage and integrity are nearly extinct, the stench of contempt insults the public nostrils, authority is arrogance, money is the dictator that can never be unseated, and you want to know why I am Lincoln?

Disenthrall yourself! Never was there a time that needed a Lincoln more!

CARLA: Come back to earth, Francis. All I want is to win a congressional election.

FRANCIS: That is not all you want.

CARLA: We're *this* close to pulling it off. We're dead even in the polls.

FRANCIS: You're three points down.

CARLA: Margin of error. One more speech will do it.

FRANCIS: Leo forbids me.

CARLA: Leo doesn't have to know.

FRANCIS: I should deceive my brother?

CARLA: You'd be helping him. And yourself.

FRANCIS: And you. Above all, and all else be damned, you need to win. Winning excuses every flaw, even your greed.

CARLA: Winning excuses your flaws, too. Admit it. You love being smarter than everybody else. And right.

(That hit the target; he looks away.)

FRANCIS: My goal is emancipation.

CARLA: Let me tell you about winning. Try losing long and hard—for like a couple of centuries—then maybe you'll see what it's worth. *(A beat)* You want to do it, Francis. One more speech. The best one yet.

(She exits. Lights change. Time passes.)

FRANCIS: "Fondly do we hope—fervently do we pray—that this mighty scourge of war may speedily pass away. Yet if God wills that it continue..."

(Enter LEO*)*

LEO: It was the best one yet. Grand and poetic. Full of ideals and hope for the future. Not one word about our opponent. Not one detail about what we would do if re-elected. It was opera. It was Shakespeare. The speech just soared above reality. And you know what? People loved it.

FRANCIS: It let them dream. What are the numbers, Leo?

LEO: We've pulled even. The race is too close to call.

(LEO exits. FRANCIS remains. The SECRETARY OF WAR *appears.)*

SECRETARY OF WAR: An exit strategy, Mister President. Always a wise idea to have one.

(He produces an empty pill bottle.)

FRANCIS: Edwin. No.

SECRETARY OF WAR: It was an accident. I was in a weakened condition from being treated like dirt. You have to back me up on that, Abe—for the insurance.

FRANCIS: Was there nothing I could do?

SECRETARY OF WAR: You did it. You were always good to me. You even made me a cabinet secretary. Thank you, Abe. *(He kisses* FRANCIS *tenderly on the cheek.)* Hey. Maybe I'll be one of those better angels of our nature.

(He exits. Transition)

Scene Three

(The scene transforms around FRANCIS. *We are in a hotel: Carpenter election headquarters. It is election night. There are noises of a rowdy crowd in the ballroom, off. Enter* LEO, *hurried, excited.)*

LEO: Francis. What are you thinking? You shouldn't be here.

FRANCIS: I can leave, Leo. I don't wish to embarrass you.

LEO: No, no, stay—but keep out of the way. I can't talk to you now, the returns are coming in.

FRANCIS: I understand.

LEO: Go in and have something to eat. But no alcohol.

FRANCIS: Very well.

LEO: And Francis, please don't talk to anyone. You know what I mean.

FRANCIS: What are the numbers?

LEO: Twenty percent of the precincts, all better than we projected. God, Francis, I think we can actually do it.

FRANCIS: Be heartened, Leo. The later precincts have an even more favorable demographic.

LEO: No, you never know. It could all fall apart, still.

FRANCIS: I predict you will be victorious by five percentage points or greater.

LEO: It's unbelievable.

FRANCIS: It is a godsend.

LEO: I have to get back in there. Please don't cause any trouble.

FRANCIS: I have purchased two bus tickets to Springfield, Leo.

LEO: Francis. Come on.

FRANCIS: Both one-way.

LEO: You can't be serious.

FRANCIS: Leo. We have an agreement.

LEO: I never agreed.

FRANCIS: That is not true. I told you I would deliver you a victory in exchange for your emancipation.

LEO: Francis, dammit. For once, I have a chance to be on the winning side. I've been on Carpenter's staff for a year and now, finally, they're starting to treat me with respect. They ask me my opinion. They introduce me to important people.

FRANCIS: None of that truly matters, Leo.

LEO: If we win tonight, it will all come together. I can't leave now.

FRANCIS: You promised.

LEO: No, you fantasized that I promised, like you fantasize everything.

FRANCIS: I am trying to help you, Leo. Don't resist me.

LEO: I am not going to be swallowed up by your needs, Francis. Not tonight.

FRANCIS: Take your ticket, Leo.

LEO: No.

FRANCIS: Please take it.

LEO: No!

FRANCIS: We'll meet at the bus station.

LEO: I am not getting on a bus with you, to Springfield or anywhere else.

FRANCIS: You're under pressure, you don't know what you're saying. *(Forcing it on him)* Here, take it. Please— just take it. *(Loudly, as if a cry for help)* Please! Please! Please!

(LEO takes it, to avoid a further public scene.)

LEO: I can't carry your weight, Francis. I have my own life to live, and that's hard enough to manage. I have to get back in there.

(He tosses the ticket to the floor and exits)

FRANCIS: You leave me no choice, Leo. I know you will forgive me.

(He picks up the bus ticket. Lights change as victory music blares and confetti falls from above; cheers from the ballroom, off, where the victory party rages... Enter CARLA *in triumph.)*

CARLA: The winner, ladies and gentlemen! This is it! This is why you do it, the feeling, like lightning and adrenaline and vodka and sex, all mixed together! Cameras and reporters and party bigs and money people, all shouting and pushing and kissing each other and spilling their drinks. *The Post* and *The Times*, front-page stories! *The Post* and *The Times*, Francis! And Dave, with this stunned look, like "We actually *won*? Now what do I do?"

FRANCIS: The impossible. Match his actions to his words.

CARLA: Dance with me, Mister President.

(She begins to dance slowly, elegantly; he mostly resists her.)

CARLA: We changed the rules, Francis. We changed how the game is played.

FRANCIS: The game is eternal. Only the players change.

CARLA: This time is different. I want to savor it. I want to glory in it... What about you, Francis? When are you going to stop letting your little brother push you around? You're the one with the gift. If you'd just stop living with one foot in a fantasy world. You need someone to help you focus, that's all.

FRANCIS: *(Anticipating her)* Someone like you.

CARLA: You're the real winner tonight. We can't keep that a secret forever. People should know—the right people. We go see Harold Daly.

FRANCIS: We?

CARLA: You do a few speeches for Harry's clients.
I help you anchor them a little.

FRANCIS: I thought you would return to the corporate
world.

CARLA: Politics is all corporate anyway. Hold me,
Francis. The whole city is wide open tonight, can't
you feel it? Anything is possible.

FRANCIS: Even Francis, returned to normal.

CARLA: Hey. We made Dave Carpenter a winner.

FRANCIS: And so we can also unmake him.

(She stops dancing, looks at him...

(Lights up on DALY *and* LEO. FRANCIS *and* CARLA *leave,
in opposite directions. She, hurriedly; he, calmly)*

DALY: So you're Leo. Francis's brother.

LEO: That's right.

DALY: And you know who I am.

LEO: Yes, sir, Mister Daly. I do.

DALY: I'm the guy who backed the loser. I hate
concession speeches. They feel like funerals.
So I came over here.

LEO: It was a well-fought campaign, sir.

DALY: It was grand larceny.

LEO: I can see how you'd say that, sir.

DALY: Dave Carpenter, raised from the dead.
Miraculous.

LEO: It seems like a miracle to us, Mister Daly, believe
me. I never thought we'd pull it off.

DALY: Me either. You never went after my man. No
personal attacks, no name-calling, no falsifying his

record. I mean, what the hell is that? You guys don't play by the rules?

LEO: You're joking, Mister Daly—aren't you?

DALY: So you must be on top of the world right now.

LEO: It feels good, I have to say, it feels really good.

DALY: The job offers will be rolling in.

LEO: Oh I don't know.

DALY: Sure they will. Everybody sucks up to the winners in this town.

(LEO *tries not to laugh*)

DALY: What.

LEO: Nobody ever called me a winner before. And nobody has ever, ever "sucked up" to me. I mean, it's funny.

DALY: So what was it, the speeches? All that ethereal shit about ideals?

LEO: That's what everybody's saying.

DALY: And you're the speech writer.

LEO: Well, there were a couple of us, you know.

DALY: So you can't take all the credit.

LEO: Not alone, no.

DALY: So Leo, tell me. What's wrong with your brother?

LEO: My brother.

DALY: Yeah. He wanders around the streets, hangs out with homeless people.

LEO: He has a paying job.

DALY: Sure, I know that. He cleans my floors. But he's an educated guy.

LEO: He has an illness.

DALY: So why would his family let him wander around like that, if he has this illness?

LEO: I'm the only family Francis has.

DALY: So I'm asking you, then. See, I think the world of Francis. But he has this breakdown, right? And he's institutionalized. Then they release him in your care. And you let him wander around the streets. I mean, what is that?

LEO: I've talked to him about it.

DALY: He's on medication?

LEO: Yes.

DALY: Which he takes every day.

LEO: Yes.

DALY: So that guy they found dead in the park— how did he end up with Francis's pills?

LEO: What guy in the park?

DALY: You know, for a top speech writer, there's a lot you're missing here, Leo.

LEO: I've been busy.

DALY: Sure, I know. So what is it? "Paranoid delusion"?

LEO: That's the official diagnosis.

DALY: Who's he think he is, again?

LEO: Lincoln.

DALY: Your brother thinks he's Abraham Lincoln.

LEO: Not all the time. I mean, he knows he's Francis, too.

DALY: And I didn't put it together until tonight. Damn, I'm stupid sometimes. It's a hell of a story.

LEO: What story?

DALY: Leo. Come on. "Congressman's Speeches Written by Madman. Author is Mental Patient Facing Charges of Drug Distribution and Uttering Racial Slurs in Public."

LEO: You can't prove that. You can't prove he wrote anything.

DALY: I don't have to. Francis told me. And I told a couple of reporters.

(Enter CARLA, *frantic but trying to hold it in.*)

CARLA: Leo. Dave wants to see you upstairs in his suite. Now.

LEO: *(To DALY)* You can't do this.

DALY: I have to disagree.

LEO: But— You said you like Francis.

DALY: Oh, I do.

LEO: Then why are you stabbing him in the back!

DALY: Rules of the game, Leo. Francis understands.

CARLA: What is this?

LEO: You fucking hypocrite!!

CARLA: He didn't mean that, Mister Daly, he's had too much to drink.

LEO: It's the hotshot assholes like you who always walk away without a scratch. You think you can have it all, don't you. Money, power, reputation.

DALY: And a happy marriage. Having it all is what this country stands for. Only whiners like you settle for less.

CARLA: You know, there's a lot of truth in that, Mister Daly.

DALY: Who the hell asked you? You better go fix your make-up, Sweetheart, you're about to get your face in the newspaper. *(To them both)* Drink up while you can, champs. There's a great big buzz saw out there about to rip your asses to shreds. Nobody comes in here and pisses in my back yard—nobody. Especially not you two losers and Dave fucking Carpenter. "Ideals." And you're telling me Francis is the crazy one? What fucking madhouse did you escape from? Here's a little lesson for you two geniuses: You never, ever let amateurs run a political campaign. It's like using children to go to war. Professional killers—that's who you want on your side. In war and politics.

(Exit DALY. LEO *and* CARLA, *stunned. Sounds of the celebration, off)*

CARLA: But we won. He can't take that away. This is a democracy, dammit!

(Exit CARLA.... *Sounds of the election night fade; lights change....)*

Scene Four

(The scene shifts to a ward in Saint Elizabeth's. LEO is alone at first. Mid-way through his lines, FRANCIS will enter slowly. He wears the uniform of an inmate in a psychiatric institution.)

LEO: The story broke the next morning. The commentary was vicious. The news media took it personally. We made them look like fools. It happened right under their noses and they didn't know... Dave fired me that same afternoon. What choice did he have? He publicly denied any knowledge of Francis, which was true. But public denial from a politician is always a sign of guilt. He held out for almost a month before he resigned.

FRANCIS: I do not think the Union will greatly miss him.

LEO: The governor named a replacement.

FRANCIS: Just as dull, just as mediocre.

LEO: Francis's trial was brief, as trials go.

FRANCIS: "Distributing a controlled substance." I am relieved that "uttering racial slurs" was dropped.

LEO: After we showed the judge that the words were straight from Lincoln.

FRANCIS: Thank you again for your testimony, Leo.

LEO: What good did it do? Here you are in this madhouse, right back where we started. Why did you insist on pleading guilty?

FRANCIS: I made a promise to my secretary of war. If a president can't keep his word, what good is he to anyone?

LEO: You're losing weight, aren't you.

FRANCIS: The food takes my appetite away.

(A beat; LEO *looks at his watch.)*

FRANCIS: Will you stay a while today, Leo?

LEO: I can't.

FRANCIS: You're busy. Have you found work?

LEO: I've got some promising leads.

FRANCIS: Have you?

LEO: No. My unemployment benefits expired last week. The rent's overdue. I'm broke.

FRANCIS: You have me. And a bus ticket to Springfield.

LEO: Great. That's just great.

FRANCIS: If only you would overcome your anger.

LEO: We had it right in our hands, everything we worked for, right in our hands. Then you went to

Harold Daly. You went directly to the enemy and gave him arms and ammunition.

FRANCIS: I acted in your best interests.

LEO: I hate it when people say that to me!

FRANCIS: I am making progress, Leo, did you know? My nurse told me.

LEO: Francis, focus. On the here and now. Can you do that?

FRANCIS: Yes.

LEO: Good.

FRANCIS: But I don't wish to. There is no profit in remaining Francis. He has so many flaws. This is my better nature.

LEO: Oh, God, Francis...

FRANCIS: I have made a choice, Leo. Don't you see how much better it is? Join me.

LEO: *(Frightened)* No!

FRANCIS: Let go. Rise up and declare it, and the city is no longer master.

LEO: Stop it, Francis.

FRANCIS: They're releasing me soon. We shall return to Illinois where we can regroup, plan a spring offensive.

LEO: Will you just fucking stop it?

FRANCIS: Please don't raise your voice, Leo.

LEO: You're not making progress. They won't let you out of here.

FRANCIS: But they will.

LEO: And I can't help you. I can't pull any strings or make any calls. I'm invisible, I'm weightless, I'm dead.

FRANCIS: Nothing is gained in despair.

LEO: Despair seems about right, if you ask me. *(He prepares to leave.)* I'll try and visit again in a few days.

FRANCIS: Leo, do you know what I think?

LEO: I have to go, Francis. *(He exits.)*

FRANCIS: I think you are an ungrateful little shit.

(A beat and LEO *enters.)*

LEO: What did you just call me?

FRANCIS: I do all to preserve the union, you do all to rend it apart. I give you freedom, you don't have the wit to use it.

LEO: This is freedom?

FRANCIS: Yes, fool! The chords that bind you are severed and what do you do? Search for more rope! And I am the one they incarcerate?

LEO: Don't you argue with me, Francis. You argue with me, you've got nobody left.

FRANCIS: Brother, must I lead you by the nose to your own salvation?

LEO: I'm not coming back here, Francis. I'm not coming back here for a long while.

FRANCIS: Neither am I. We are both going to Springfield.

*(*LEO *hangs his head in exasperation: there's no arguing with this madman.)*

FRANCIS: Meanwhile I shall keep your bus ticket right here, in this envelope from Harry.

LEO: That bastard again. He comes out of this fatter than ever, and look at us.

FRANCIS: I also have your teaching certificate here.

LEO: My what?

FRANCIS: When you're ready. There is no hurry. You are now certified in Illinois. Grades K through 12.

LEO: I didn't apply for a teaching certificate.

(DALY *enters.*)

DALY: I was acting in your best interests.

FRANCIS: Harry has friends in Illinois.

DALY: I have friends basically everywhere.

FRANCIS: There's also a letter here for you—from Miss Rourke.

DALY: She's writing a book.

LEO: Carla? A book about what?

(CARLA *enters.*)

CARLA: A Capitol Hill staffer who thinks he's Abraham Lincoln.

FRANCIS: Based on a true story.

LEO: What is this?

DALY: The lady needs a quiet place to write. Preferably way out of town.

CARLA: Harry thought Springfield would be ideal.

FRANCIS: I have to say, I agree. I think I am too much a burden upon you, Leo. With Miss Rourke, you would have someone to talk to when I am at work.

LEO: At work.

DALY: Costumed interpreter.

FRANCIS: At the Lincoln Tomb State Historic Site.

LEO: Are you telling me—?

FRANCIS: (*Joyous*) I shall be Lincoln! Officially! And they will pay me for it! I shall even have a stovepipe hat. Think how good I shall be in a stovepipe hat.

LEO: *(To* DALY*)* But how did you—?

FRANCIS: Harry has—

LEO: —"friends in Illinois." Right.

DALY: It's in his best interests.

FRANCIS: But we must never mention Harry's name.

DALY: Ever—which is in my best interests. Francis is a dangerous influence. Better for him to relocate for a while. Politically, he was just too far ahead of his time.

FRANCIS: I don't think our present is quite ready for the past.

LEO: Wait a minute here. *(To* CARLA*)* You? A book?

CARLA: Harry was telling me: every good Washington scandal has a book in it.

DALY: Rules of the game.

CARLA: I was thinking you could help me. I'm having a little writer's block.

LEO: What happened to the corporate career?

CARLA: After the excitement of the campaign and all—corporate's too sane for me. Besides: next time? *(Rapidly)* We jump out to an early lead then we use the Internet to build massive grassroots financial support and hey, did you ever take a look at the speeches of Thomas Jefferson?

DALY: *(A warning)* Carla.

FRANCIS: Miss Rourke. Have we learned nothing?

CARLA: *(Back to sobriety)* Right. Sorry.

LEO: You know, maybe it's this hospital, but... I think *I'm* the one who's going crazy.

(They all hold their arms out to LEO*.)*

FRANCIS: Join us, Leo, and your emancipation will be complete.

LEO: A teacher. You know... I think I'd be good at teaching.

(LEO, CARLA *and* DALY *turn slowly, their smiles gone, and stare directly at the audience. They remain motionless, figures of Francis's fantasy.* FRANCIS *comes downstage and now addresses the great gathering.*)

FRANCIS: Citizens. "I am loath to close. We are not enemies, but friends. We must not be enemies. Though passion may have strained, it must not break our bonds of affection. The mystic chords of memory, stretching from every battle-field, and patriot grave—"

(CARLA *steps forward now as a doctor in a white lab coat. She carries a chart.*)

DOCTOR: That was very good, Francis.

FRANCIS: I wasn't done.

DOCTOR: Is there anyone in the room with us, Francis?

FRANCIS: No.

DOCTOR: No?

FRANCIS: My brother.

DOCTOR: Your brother is outside in the hallway.

FRANCIS: He is?

DOCTOR: We were discussing your medication.

FRANCIS: I do not need medication.

DOCTOR: I will ask again: Is there anyone else in the room with us?

FRANCIS: Perhaps. One or two.

DOCTOR: Good. I wish you would trust me more.

FRANCIS: I wish you would be someone worthy of my trust.

(LEO *joins the* DOCTOR *as she makes a note on her chart.*)

LEO: He seems better today.

DOCTOR: There are signs of progress.

LEO: There are?

DOCTOR: He still has imaginary visitors, though. Carries on long discussions with them.

(*Here* DALY *gives* FRANCIS *a warm hug and exits.*)

DOCTOR: On the other hand, Francis has organized a debate club on the ward. The other patients enjoy it—but he does tend to dominate.

LEO: Doctor Barlow?

DOCTOR: Yes?

LEO: I've been having a rough time finding a job, after the election scandal—a job in politics, I mean. I've decided to try teaching school. Francis always wanted that for me.

DOCTOR: He'll be pleased.

LEO: Will he be let out? Eventually?

DOCTOR: I think so. Eventually.

LEO: I'm so worried about him, in here alone. We promised to stick together.

DOCTOR: He's not alone. Francis has a very rich imaginary world. He's probably much happier than you or I. (*She exits.*)

LEO: Francis. I have to go.

FRANCIS: Godspeed, Leo. All will end happily. We need only have faith in the union.

LEO: I'm sorry. For everything, I'm so sorry.

FRANCIS: All has been forgiven, long ago.

LEO: I love you, Francis.

FRANCIS: I love you too, brother. We'll leave for Springfield soon. But I have so much work to do here first. All the many wounded. A nation at war with itself.

LEO: Goodbye. And... God keep you, Mister President.

(FRANCIS smiles benevolently at his brother, who exits. After a beat, FRANCIS returns to the task at hand: his presidential address.)

FRANCIS: "We must not be enemies. Though passion may have strained, it must not break our bonds of affection. The mystic chords of memory, stretching from every battle-field, and patriot grave, to every living heart and hearthstone, all over this broad land, will yet swell the chorus of the Union, when again touched, as surely they will be, by the better angels of our nature."

(Lights)

END OF PLAY

References to Lincoln's speeches used in the play

ACT ONE, Scene One.

"If we could first know where we are, and wither we are tending, we could better judge what to do, and how to do it.

We are now in the fifth year, since a policy was initiated, with the avowed object, and confident promise, of putting an end to slavery agitation.

Under the operation of that policy, the agitation has not only not ceased, but it has constantly augmented.

In my opinion, it will not cease, until a crisis shall have been reached, and passed.

A house divided against itself cannot stand.

I believe this government cannot endure, permanently half slave and half free.

I do not expect the union to be dissolved—I do not expect the house to fall-but I do expect it will cease to be divided.

It will become all one thing, or all the other.

The result is not doubtful. We shall not fail-if we stand firm, we shall not fail.

Wise counsels may accelerate or mistakes delay it, but sooner or later the victory is sure to come."

—From the "House Divided" speech, Springfield, Ill., Republican State Convention, June 16, 1858.

ACT ONE, Scene Four

Couch and Smith, Stanton! Why am I plagued with Couch and Smith? Smith took ten days to move his

army from Carlisle to Hagerstown. That's not an inch over fifty-five miles, if so much. While General Meade, with twenty thousand veteran troops, sits by and lets Lee's army build bridges over the river and slip away at his leisure without attacking him. I believe you do not appreciate the magnitude of the misfortune involved in Lee's escape. [...] He was within our easy grasp and to have closed upon him would have ended the war. Now the war will be prolonged indefinitely. [...] Our golden opportunity is gone, and I am distressed immeasurably because of it.
—From a draft of a letter to General Meade (*paraphrased*), July 14, 1863.

ACT ONE, Scene Six.
    "The world has never had a good definition of the word liberty, and the American people, just now, are in much want of one. We all declare for liberty; in using the same word, we do not all mean the same thing. With some, the word liberty may mean for each man to do as he pleases with himself and the product of his labor; while with others the word may mean for men to do as they please with other men, and the product of other men's labor. Each of these things is called by two different and incompatible names—liberty and tyranny."
—Address at a "Sanitary Fair" in Baltimore, April 18, 1864

ACT ONE, Scene Eight
    "We say we are for the union. The world will not forget that we say this. We know how to save the Union. The world knows we do know how to save it. We hold the power and bear the responsibility. In giving freedom to the slave, we assure freedom to the free—honorable alike in what we give, and what we preserve... The way is plain, generous, just—a way the world will forever applaud, and God must forever

bless."
—Annual message to Congress, December 1, 1863

ACT TWO, Scene Two
  "The dogmas of the quiet past are inadequate to the stormy present."
—Annual message to Congress, December 1, 1863

ACT TWO, Scene Two
  "The fiery trial through which we pass will light us down, in honor or dishonor, to the latest generation."
—Annual message to Congress, December 1, 1863

ACT TWO, Scene Three
  "Fondly do we hope—fervently do we pray—that this mighty scourge of war may speedily pass away. Yet if God wills that it continue..."
—Second Inaugural Address, March 4, 1865

  "With malice toward none; with charity for all; with firmness in the right, as God gave us to see the right, let us strive on to finish the work we are in; to bind up the nation's wounds; to care for him who shall have borne the battle, and for his widow, and his orphan-to do all which may achieve and cherish a just and lasting peace, among ourselves, and with all nations."
—Second Inaugural Address, March 4, 1865

ACT TWO, Scene Five
  "I am loath to close. We are not enemies, but friends. We must not be enemies. Though passion may have strained, it must not break our bonds of affection. The mystic chords of memory, stretching from every battle-field, and patriot grave, to every living heart and hearthstone, all over this broad land, will yet swell the chorus of the Union, when again touched, as surely they will be, by the better angels of our nature."
—First Inaugural Address, March 4, 1861

www.ingramcontent.com/pod-product-compliance
Lightning Source LLC
Chambersburg PA
CBHW052159090426
42741CB00010B/2329